mostly

A KIDS' GUIDE TO

SECOND EDITION

NAPLES, MARCO ISLAND
AND THE EVERGLADES

Karen T. Bartlett

*Dedicated to all the great kids on these pages
and those we've met along the way.
Thanks for being awesome!*

Inspired by the **never-ending story** of
adventure and **discovery** with the **loves of my life,**
Christopher Y. Bartlett and Sarah Rose Bartlett

Lead Designer: Jayla Buie
Design Associate: Brad Sanders
Illustrators: Margie Olsen, Terri Rickman Golden
Cover Design: Christine Rooney
Regional photos by Karen T. Bartlett except where otherwise credited
Content Advisors: Sarah R. Bartlett, Christopher Y. Bartlett
Research and Editorial Assistants: Brenna Ulrich, Kira Pirre, Randall Simmons
Proofreader: Lyn Hunter, PhD

To schedule an event or inquire about volume discounts, contact
Karen@mostlykidsguides.com (239) 595–9026

 @kidsguides Mostly Kids Guides
www.mostlykidsguides.com

ISBN 978-0-9909731-2-6

DISCLAIMER

The text in this book is strictly editorial, not advertising, included at the whim of the author, based on her experiences, impressions, research, and gleanings from local legends for the enjoyment of children and their families. It is not intended as a comprehensive guide, nor should it be taken as a definitive scientific, historic, or geographic authority. Mostly Kids' Guides expressly disclaims liability for any errors or omissions.

Events, attractions and resources are always subject to change. To avoid disappointment, check ahead for the latest information.

IMAGES BY SHUTTERSTOCK

We had so much fun sprinkling artful pirates, creatures and footprints, beach and sports symbols and tasty treats across the pages of this book. All these, unless otherwise credited, as well as the awesome polka dots, splashes and confetti, are provided by Shutterstock.

Are there **ghosts** in the **swamp?** Have you ever seen a **creature** with a **tongue longer than your arm,** or a blade of grass higher than a house? **Do trees have knees?** And what in the world is a **swamp buggy?** Well, here's the **inside scoop** on stuff that's almost **too bizarre** to be true. **But it is!**

"And wait till you see what else!"

WHAT'S INSIDE?

Stuff you Need to Know. Some of it is quite weird!

Giant Blade of Grass!

Can you believe it? A palm tree isn't really a tree! It's a gigantic blade of grass! It's a bit more complicated than that, but it's true! Palm trees are actually related to onions and the grass in your garden.

Shell Trees? For Real?

Get close and you'll see what's really going on here! Certain sea snails drill holes in small shells to slurp out the animal inside. Some people say that if you hang a shell on a mangrove tree at your favorite beach, you're sure to come back some day.

Tweezers & Spoons

Here's a good way to figure out the birds on the beach.

Shore birds, like sandpipers and plovers, are little guys that skitter along the water's edge, poking in the sand for tasty treats.

Wading birds, like ibis and herons, have long necks and long skinny legs. They fish with sharp, pointy beaks like tweezers.

*"We roseate spoonbills are wading birds, but instead of tweezers, we scoop up our food with the **handy spoon** at the end of our beaks!"*

Sea birds, like gulls and pelicans, don't have tweezers or spoons. They swoop down and dive for their dinner.

tweezer beak

COWABUNGA! It's a Manatee!

Cousins!

In ancient times, **pirates and explorers** saw manatees and thought they were **mermaids**. We sometimes call them **sea cows**. Why? Because they're **fat and cow-like!** Also, they chew grass. Sea grass, that is. **Manatees move very slowly** (you might too, if you weighed almost **2,000 pounds!**), so their worst **enemies are boat propellers**.

This is Ariel

She's the Mostly Kids' Tribe's very own **adopted manatee**. She's as **beautiful as a mermaid,** don't you think?

"Yes, she is!"
"Did you know they're not related to any sea creatures? But they ARE related to elephants!"

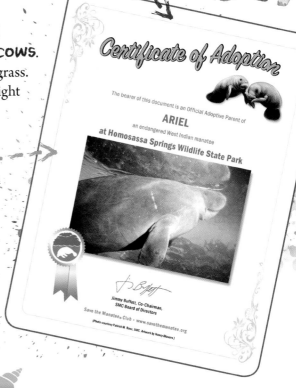

Certificate of Adoption

The bearer of this document is an Official Adoptive Parent of

ARIEL

an endangered West Indian manatee

at Homosassa Springs Wildlife State Park

Jimmy Buffett, Co-Chairman,
SMC Board of Directors

Save the Manatee Club • www.savethemanatee.org

(Photo courtesy Patrick M. Rose, SMC. Artwork by Nancy Blauers.)

Live fighting conch sticking its face out to see what's going on.

Live shelling: Don't do it!

You'll find lots of **pretty shells** on the beach. If you find one with the **creature still inside,** or a sea star that's still soft—even if it's washed up on the beach and not feeling well— don't take it! Live shells out of water die and get **really smelly**. Also, it's against the law. **Empty shells are fine to take!**

"Even if the creature is already dead and stinky, still don't take it! Why not? It's dinner for us crabs and also birds!"

5

Prehistoric Sea Turtles Invade the Beaches!

Every spring, **ginormous loggerhead sea turtles** swim to the same beaches where they were born to lay their eggs. They **crawl out of the sea at night** and use their **huge flippers** to dig nests. It's very hard work for the mother turtle. When she hatched, she weighed only **one ounce**. Now she weighs about **300 pounds!**

Afterward, she crawls **v-e-r-y slowly** back to the sea. Every morning, during the **nesting months** of May to October, turtle specialists patrol the beaches and mark the nests with yellow tape.

Flipper tracks look like monster tire tracks!

Markus Hennig

Turtle specialist rescues babies stuck in the nest.

You won't believe what happens next! All the babies hatch at the same time! They **erupt like a volcano** out of the nest and trip all over each other to get to the sea. They run as fast as their tiny legs can take them to the sea, because crabs and birds love to eat them for breakfast.

Everyone loves the **turtle biologists!** Come to the beach early one morning during nesting time and watch them work!

When a **baby girl turtle** grows up, in about 35 years, she'll swim back **thousands of miles** (from other oceans, even!) to lay her eggs. How can she remember the exact beach where she was born?

It's a mystery!

Boardwalk Secrets

Boardwalks help protect the swamps, beaches, preserves and prairies. Look down and see what might be looking up at you! Maybe a gopher tortoise!

A gopher tortoise is NOT a sea turtle!

Gopher tortoises have been around almost since dinosaurs—over 60 **MILLION YEARS**! They can't live in the water, and they pretty much don't like the taste of it, either.

Best digger ever! A gopher tortoise lives in a long, **deep burrow** in the sand—as long as a school bus!—and doesn't mind sharing it with hundreds of other kinds of creatures, like **mice and snakes**. It must be safe because gopher tortoises can live to be **100 years old**!

Not vegetarian.
Loves seafood.

Vegetarian.
Loves flowers, grass and berries.

Going Fishing?

Kids under 16, Florida grownups over 65, and people fishing with licensed guides **don't need a fishing license**. Everyone can fish without a license from the Naples Pier, and all Florida residents can fish from the beach for free. *Everybody else: get a license!*

BLUE ZONES PROJECT

Who wants to be blue? We do!

Some people say that if you're blue, that means you're sad, but not here! No way! Besides our really, really blue sky (just look up!), there's more to being a Blue Zones community, and we're working on becoming one. How? By eating more dee-licious, healthier kinds of food, **going outside more to play**, and **making new friends**. When you go to a restaurant, you may see some Blue Zones Project-inspired choices on the menu. Mmm good!

Freaky Factoids!

What happens when you chase a flock of gulls?

Making them fly up in a rush to get away gets them **so tired** that they sometimes **can't fish.** So please don't do it!

"Key limes make yellow juice, not green! I should know, because **I'm a Pie-Rat.** *Get it?"*

One foot?

NOT!

Do you ever see a sea bird **hopping around like it has only one foot?** Well guess what! Most of the time, the other foot is **tucked up** there in the feathers. It helps them to **save energy!**

Sometimes a bigger bird does get tangled up in a **fishing line** and can lose a foot or leg. If you see a fishing line, or a **straw** or **piece of a balloon** or any **plastic thing** on the beach that creatures might think is food, **be a creature hero** and an **environmentalist.** Toss it in the trash. You can save a life!

*"Did you know that **plastic bags** look like **delicious jellyfish** to us birds, dolphins, and sea turtles?"*

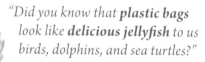

Jellyfish!

Imagine This!

All the straws used in America in one day could fill **127 school buses.**

Please don't take plastic straws to the beach!

Please don't eat green sea grapes!
(Unless they're **ripe**, in a jar of purple sea grape jelly.)

Some say that **pirates used their daggers** to scrape secret messages into the leaves. **Try it!**

"But not with a dagger, arrr! Use a pointy shell!"

Yum!

The letters will turn white at first, and then disappear in a few days.

Want to be a Junior Ranger?

JUNIOR RANGER · EXPLORE · LEARN · PROTECT ·

Kids of all ages can sign up for free at any state or national park for cool ranger programs, activities & fun stuff!

Don't eat these oats, either!
(They're way too **scratchy!**)

Besides, sea oats help save sand dunes from washing away into the sea, so picking them is against the law!

RAPTORS!

Bald Eagle

Great, great (a gazillion great) GRANDCHILDREN of DINOSAURS!

And guess what! They still have **dinosaur super-powers.** A bald eagle can dive for fish at 100 miles per hour!

How can you tell the difference between an osprey and an eagle?

Bald eagles have white heads and **yellow beaks.** Ospreys have black and white heads and **black beaks.**

It's easy to spot the sticks of osprey nests in dead tree branches and on channel markers. Eagles' nests need **big strong trees** because they are HUMONGOUS: Maybe bigger than your bed!

Osprey

Q: Why does a snowy egret wear yellow slippers?

A: That's easy! It wiggles its spiky yellow toes in the water to freak out the fish, and then snatches some up for lunch!

38

Both ospreys and bald eagles **eat mostly fish,** it's true. But eagles also love snakes, frogs, mice and vulture vomit.

Disgusting!

Ancient Indians & Dastardly Pirates

Way before the Seminole Indians and Spanish Conquistadors, and before English pirates sailed here looting treasure ships, lived the **Calusa Indians, the fiercest warriors** in **Florida history.** Ponce de Leon made a **HUGE MISTAKE** when he tried to conquer the Calusas. They killed him with a **poison arrow!**

The Calusa also were **very smart pirates!** They ambushed Spanish galleons. Sea captains **told their queen** that the Calusa were **giants and cannibals.** Maybe that was just a **lame excuse** for showing up without any treasure.

Calico Jack's Gold

When a hurricane tossed the ship of that **dastardly pirate, Calico Jack,** right into the **Ten Thousand Islands,** what did he find? A **wrecked treasure ship,** loaded with **300,000 gold coins!** He **buried the gold,** but he **never came back** to dig it up!

Treasure on Panther Key?

When **Jose Gaspar's** pirate ship got captured, only a cabin boy named **Juan Gomez** escaped. Did he know about **Calico Jack's treasure?** The boy camped on one of the Ten Thousand Islands and grew up as a **hermit,** fishing and raising goats. He named his island **Panther Key** because panthers kept swimming over to **eat his goats.** He lived to age 122, but he **never found the treasure.**

Some believe all that **gold is still there,** waiting to be discovered. **Maybe by you!**

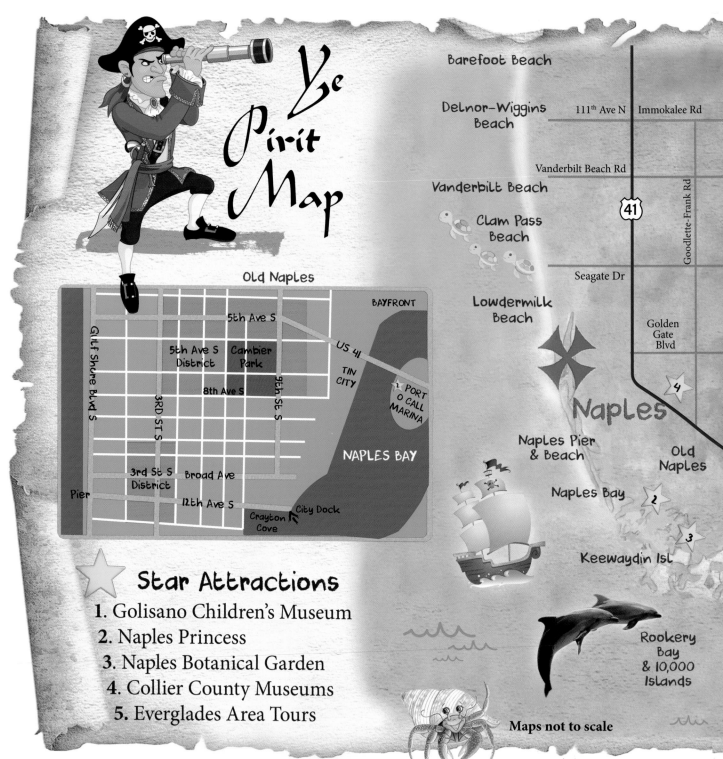

Ye Pirit Map

Barefoot Beach

Delnor-Wiggins Beach

111th Ave N | Immokalee Rd

Vanderbilt Beach Rd

41

Goodlette-Frank Rd

Vanderbilt Beach

Clam Pass Beach

Seagate Dr

Lowdermilk Beach

Golden Gate Blvd

Old Naples

BAYFRONT

5th Ave S

US 41

TIN CITY

PORT O CALL MARINA

5th Ave S District

Cambier Park

Gulf Shore Blvd S

3RD ST S

8th Ave S

9th St S

NAPLES BAY

3rd St S District

Broad Ave

Pier

12th Ave S

City Dock

Crayton Cove

Naples

Naples Pier & Beach

Old Naples

Naples Bay

2

3

Keewaydin Isl

Rookery Bay & 10,000 Islands

Maps not to scale

Star Attractions

1. Golisano Children's Museum
2. Naples Princess
3. Naples Botanical Garden
4. Collier County Museums
5. Everglades Area Tours

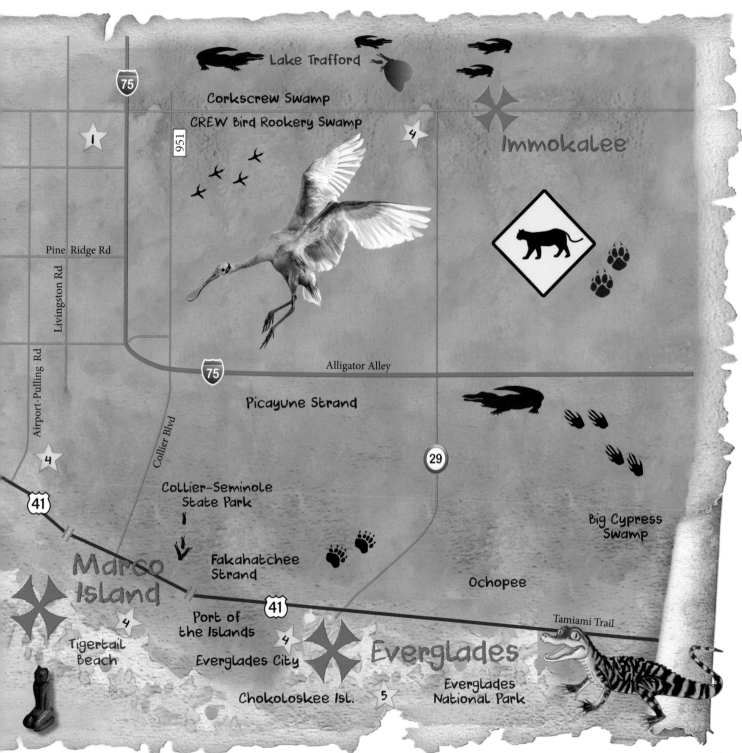

Lake Trafford

Corkscrew Swamp

CREW Bird Rookery Swamp

Immokalee

Pine Ridge Rd

Livingston Rd

Airport-Pulling Rd

Collier Blvd

Alligator Alley

Picayune Strand

Collier-Seminole
State Park

Big Cypress
Swamp

Marco
Island

Fakahatchee
Strand

Ochopee

Port of
the Islands

Tamiami Trail

Tigertail
Beach

Everglades City

Everglades

Chokoloskee Isl.

Everglades
National Park

Sooo Many Beaches!

When your bare toes squiggle in the **soft sand** for the very first time, you might say, "Whoa! These are the most splendiferous beaches in America." And you'd be RIGHT!

What would you like to do today? Build a **sand castle?** Look for shells and sea stars? Fly your **kite?** Toss a **Frisbee?** Sit oh-so-quietly and watch a pelican take a bath, or splash around in the water yourself? And **which beach to choose?** Easy! After you've played yourself silly on one, just head over to the next!

QUIZ
What should you feed a sea bird?
a. a bite of a hotdog
b. bread crusts
c. shrimp
d. bacon
e. none of these

Answer: e. people food makes birds sick.

Is that bacon?

*"Certainly **not!** It's sea grass!"*

The Beach at the Pier

Q. What's the number one rule for Naples visitors?
A. You have to go all the way to the end of the Naples Pier to watch the sun set.

Well, we made that up, but it would be really sad if you don't! Dolphins, **sea birds,** and even **manatees** love to hang out around the pier. Sometimes the fishermen even catch a **shark.** Check out those ospreys that rule the roof!

Your **pooch** on a **leash** can walk on the pier but is not allowed on the beach. There's beach volleyball for older kids and a **snack stand** right on the pier.

Hey kids! You can borrow a life jacket for free at The Naples Pier, Clam Pass, Vanderbilt Beach and other county beaches.

Lowdermilk Beach Park

You're sure to make new friends on this super family-friendly beach, which also has **playgrounds,** sand volleyball, a big covered **food pavilion** and shady picnic tables.

It's a great place for a **birthday party!**

Naples Kayak, **Old Naples Surf Shop** and others deliver kayaks and paddleboards right to you at **Lowdermilk** and several other beaches.

Clam Pass Park

You get to ride the free beach tram through a real mangrove forest to get to this beach! There's a snack deck and beach equipment to rent. Walk north to Clam Pass to check out the huuuge flocks of pelicans and gulls.

Vanderbilt Beach Park

This is another famous beach to see the sunset. But why wait? It's great for swimming, making sand sculptures, and playing all day! Check out Naples Beach Watersports for Waverunners, parasailing other fun adventures. Cabana Dan's has ice cream, sunscreen, paddleboats, umbrellas and other important stuff. More food and shops are just outside the park.

Blow me a Kiss, Jellyfish!

Of course you can't be at the beach ALL the time, right? Sometimes you want to say 'bye to sand, shells, and sea creatures and go splash in the pool, see a movie, or go on one of the adventures in this book! And guess what! The Collier County Public Library has different fun goings-on every month at all their branches. Like family storytimes, craft days, and even Pups 'n' Books days when you can read a story to a puppy. For real! — or just pet one!

Delnor-Wiggins Pass State Park

Bring your fishing pole!

You'll cross the **sand dunes** on **boardwalks** to get to this mile-long beach. There are **shady spots** with tables and grills, food concessions, **kayak** and **paddleboard** rentals, and beach umbrellas. Cool tours and free ranger activities, too! Go to the very end and climb the **lookout tower.**

Green Flash?
A bright green glow sometimes happens when the last tip of the setting sun drops into the sea. It's very fast but lots of people have seen it. Maybe you will!

Smart Kid Alert: never stare into the sun!

"Don't forget to put on sunscreen!"

Barefoot Beach Preserve Park

Go on a free adventure with a ranger, kayak through the **mangrove swamps** where manatees live, look for tiny sea creatures in the sea grass beds and **mud flats,** watch shore birds fishing for their lunch, have lunch yourself, play on the **big sandy beach,** find some shells and splash in the water. And then what? Start all over again!

The Beach at Lake Avalon

Is there a fresh water lake around here? Yes! On Lake Avalon at **Sugden Regional Park,** you can rent a paddleboat, ride bikes around the lake, **fish on the pier,** and see what's flitting around the butterfly garden. There are **sailing** and water skiing classes for kids (and grownups) with all abilities, **picnic shelters** with **grills** right on the beach, and a **playground,** too.

There's a GINORMOUS ice cream social on the 4th of July with games, **ski shows** and **fireworks,** and in the fall comes the AMAZIFYING **Pro Watercross World Championships!** Both are FREE!

Island Beaches

Keewaydin Island & Cape Romano

The **birds and creatures** on these islands outnumber the people about **two bazillion to one!** There's nothing to do here except **find shells** and swim and play. Well, there **IS** something **very weird** in the **water** on **Cape Romano**. The **mystery** is **solved** in the Marco Island chapter.

At lunchtime, **snack** and **ice cream** boats come sailing right up to **Keewaydin** beach. And guess what! Keewaydin is the **only beach** in the whole county where you can **bring your dog!**

Woo hoo!

No bridges! If you're not a bird or sea creature, you must hop aboard a **sightseeing boat** in Naples or Marco Island to get to these two islands. You could even rent a **Jet Ski** or **pontoon boat**.

Keewaydin

Cape Romano

Marco Island Beaches

There are **no tigers** at all on **Tigertail Beach**—or any tiger tails lying around, either, which is **excellent news**. The other excellent news is that **you don't need a boat** to get there! **Get the scoop** in the Marco Island chapter.

NAPLES Oh, the Fun You'll Have on Land & Sea

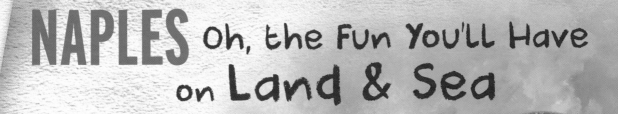

So now you know that wherever you are in Naples, you're always near a beach. Guess what! You also can **climb a tree house** just like in the movies, **feed a giraffe**, sail on a **fancy yacht**, go down a **water slide** or ride a kid-size **steam train**. You can laugh your head off at a **silly play**, go deep-sea fishing, meet a gopher tortoise — or even BE ONE!

What else? You can **ride your bike** through creature habitats, **ride a pony** through the forest, go to a **festival**, jump in a foam pit, and, oh, **a gazillion other things!**

try this yourself at C'mon Golisano Children's Museum of Naples

Anteaters to Zebras: Zoo-rific!

What's up at the **Naples Zoo**? Besides the giraffes, that is. They're WAY up there! But they love to bend down and **eat yummy lettuce** right out of your hand! There's a **boat ride** around the primate islands, where apes, monkeys and lemurs hang out. You'll **giggle at the bears** having lunch at their picnic table. There's serious **chomping action** in Alligator Bay at feeding time, and fun shows in the Safari Canyon theater. You can get nose-to-nose with Lions and tigers (through a glass, of course) and get almost nose-to-nose with **vipers** and **rattlesnakes** (with no glass!) at Snakes Alive!

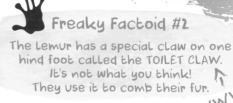

Freaky Factoid #2
The Lemur has a special claw on one hind foot called the TOILET CLAW. It's not what you think! They use it to comb their fur.
EWWW!

Freaky Factoid #1
A giraffe's **tongue** is **black** and R-E-A-L-L-Y Long! But not as Long as the anteater's. It's two feet Long!

Yay! An Easter egg hunt!

Giraffes have knobby knees!

Zebra Longwing
It's Florida's state butterfly. The name fits, don't you think?

Garden-Licious

Whoever said a garden is just a bunch of flowers was **WRONG!** At least not this one! Here are some **fun things** you can do at **Naples Botanical Garden**: Get wet in the **splash fountain**. Climb an awesome **tree house**. Draw on the chalk art sidewalk. Crawl around on a pretend spider web. Visit a **cave** and waterfall. Build a sand castle. Look for deer and wading birds from the **birding tower**. Discover so many **bizarre things** that are definitely **NOT** flowers in the **Hidden Garden**, including a **toilet clogged** with **flowers**. For real! See for yourself!

The **Cracker House** is a cool **kid-size playhouse**. In its garden you can **plant flowers, dig weeds, or water** the **organic vegetables**. Pay attention, because **surprises are everywhere!** Can you spot the **tree** wearing **striped socks?**

More Fun Things To Do

Sit very still in the **Butterfly House**, and a butterfly might **land on your nose!**

Drop in any Saturday or Sunday morning and be a **W.O.N.D.E.R. kid**. They have a whole bunch of fun new adventures and activities every month. **Even grownups love it!**

Dogs have their own **private entrance** three days a week. They love sniffing all those **grass and creature smells** (everywhere except the shop, cafe, or children's garden), and **they get treats, too!**

QUIZ
Butterflies taste their food with:

a. their tongues, silly
b. tiny forks
c. their feet

Answer: c (that's the truth!)

Wild Creature Hospital and other SPLENDIFEROUS Things!

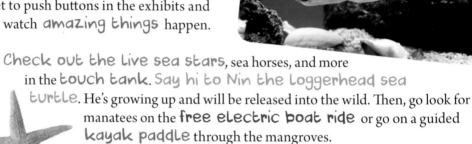

All kinds of cuddly, freaky (and sometimes creepy) critters live at the Conservancy of Southwest Florida. You can peek into the hospital for injured wildlife and orphaned baby animals, and meet animal ambassadors of all kinds. In the Dalton Discovery Center, you get to push buttons in the exhibits and watch amazing things happen.

Check out the live sea stars, sea horses, and more in the touch tank. Say hi to Nin the Loggerhead sea turtle. He's growing up and will be released into the wild. Then, go look for manatees on the free electric boat ride or go on a guided kayak paddle through the mangroves.

Aliens?

Well, sort of, because they don't belong here in Florida! In the Hallway of Invasive Species you might spot an **ugly cane toad** or a **beautiful lionfish**.

Hop on the Trolley!

What's-what and what's-where in Naples? Hop aboard and find out! The tour guides tell hilarious secrets about Naples people, places and creatures. You can hop off (and back on) at any stop for an adventure, lunch or souvenir shopping.

Little Kids Alert!

Head for the Little Explorers Play Zone for stories, nature crafts and fun! Meet Dr. Ollie Owl, the veterinarian, and even be a junior veterinarian yourself!

PUSHART

C'mon! PLAY and Learn!

Where can you go to be an architect, a veterinarian, or a trolley driver, cook in a pretend restaurant, paint in an art studio, or catch a fish at a pretend pier? Why, at Golisano Children's Museum of Naples (C'mon), of course!

But that's not all! At C'mon, you can climb a giant banyan tree and see a gator in the pretend swamp. There's even a pretend tropical storm in the Everglades – thunder, lightning and all! In Mother Nature's House, you can be a meteorologist in the TV studio, rake up falling autumn leaves, and hang out in an igloo with ice walls! In Backyardville, you can do fun things like roll down a grassy hill and make a splash at the water play table.

BUILD IT! is really fun

Whoa! C'mon is supposed to be for kids, but who are they fooling? Your grownups will have a blast!

It's cold in here!

ADULTS KEEP OUT of **Curious Kids,** where teens and pre-teens do mysterious scientific experiments, invent, design and build awesome things. Little kids have their own play lot!

Sensory Night! One night each month, sounds and lights are dimmed for the enjoyment of kids with sensory limitations.

Mini Wonders Workshops

Elephant toothpaste? A sneeze tissue for a flea? Butter-making? There's always an awesome new activity especially for little learners ages 2–5.

23

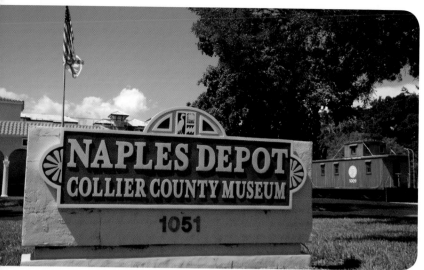

Trains, Tanks

*"What's a depot? ye might ask. It's a building to wait for yer train, if ye didn't have a **pie-rat** ship, arrr."*

100 years ago this place was a **real train depot.** Now, it's a **museum** for all kinds of old-time transportation, like a **Seminole dugout canoe**, a **pioneer mule wagon**, a really old **swamp buggy**, a **1955 Chevy** Bel Air car, and even the nose of an **Army Air Force plane**. Be sure to take a selfie at the **100 year-old red caboose!**

Admission is free at **Naples Depot Museum & The Collier Museum at Government Center!**

ALL Aboard!

Fun birthday adventure!

Hop aboard the **mini-train**, pulled by a real **kid-size diesel locomotive** at the **Naples Train Museum**. It's at the other end of the Depot building. Check ahead for rates and schedules. Inside, you can watch **Thomas the Tank** and other miniature **Lionel trains** chug around the model city. Push buttons and **watch cool things happen!**

and Giant Saber-toothed Cats!

Want to find out about **prehistoric saber-toothed cats, mastodons** and other creatures that roamed around Florida a zillion years ago? You can, at the **Collier Museum at Government Center.** You also can see **Indian weapons,** visit the **archaeology lab** and check out lots of cool **interactive exhibits.**

Outside, there's a **Log fort,** Seminole chickees, and a huuuge **World War II Sherman tank.** But that's not all, no sir and no ma'am. Kids especially love **Old Number 2,** the cypress swamp **steam locomotive,** and the old-time **swamp buggies.** There are nice **shady paths** and **picnic spots,** too!

Old Number 2 Locomotive

Photos (3) colliermuseums.org

Zoom back in history for real!

Come to **Stories of the Paradise Coast** in November. It's a super-fun **family weekend** with **kids' activities and crafts,** actors and **storytellers,** food and surprises. How much is the admission? **Zero!**

Q. What's SUP?
A. Stand Up Paddleboarding!

It's **sooo much fun** and **easy** to learn. Practice in quiet places where **dolphins** and **manatees** live, like the **hidden lagoons** and bays of the Cocohatchee River. Check out the tours and rentals at **AWE All Water Excursions**. Would you rather kayak? Sign up for **Mike Devlin's** one and only "**Mini Ten Thousand Islands**" **Ecotour** with **secret passages** through the mangroves.

She's just learning! →

Dive! Snorkel! Fish the Reef!

If you don't have natural coral reefs, what do you do? Build some! We have **18,000 tons** of artificial reefs made out of **old boats, steel poles** and even **concrete houses.** For real! And we have lots of **fishing guides** to take you there. Check out the **kids' scuba programs** and camps at **Scuba Outfitters Naples.**

"The best reef is in the shape of me—a giant sea turtle! New baby coral and sponge are already growing on it, and the fish are so happy!"

Secret Passage!

Mike Devlin

important objects

Learn Some History!

With letters, artifacts, family pictures and stories, **The Holocaust Museum and Education Center** helps us understand Hitler's horrible Nazi war crimes, so that such things are never allowed to happen again. Take a public or **private family tour.**

In Europe, a **100-year-old house** is practically new. But in Naples, that's **ancient!** When pioneers built **Palm Cottage** near the Naples Pier in 1895 using crushed sand and seashells, Naples wasn't even born yet. Now **it's a museum.** It's especially pretty when it's all decorated for the holidays.

Slide! Zoom! Plume & Flume!

If you've been to a more exciting water park than Sun-N-Fun Lagoon, it was probably on another planet. Check out the water-dumping buckets, water pistols, four pools, lazy river, and five water slides. Kids 5 to 12, head for Turtle Cove. Little kids get their very own tadpole pool.

"Do ye dare try the big tower? Ye have to be 48 inches high."

Collier County Parks & Recreation

Can U Dig It?

Sun-N-Fun Lagoon is at North Collier Regional Park, which also has a big playground with slides, swings, big rocks to climb, squiggly poles and climbing structures. There's even a Calusa fossil dig!

Taste Something Yummy!

Bees just love our mangrove flowers! At the weekend farm markets, you can taste mangrove honey and other yummy samples like mac 'n' cheese or gluten-free muffins! Most months, especially October to May, there's music, pet treats and art-i-ful souvenirs.

Swamp Buggy Races
Muck, Mud and the Sippy Hole!

It's not a truck, a motorcycle, a racecar, an airplane or a boat. So, what in the world IS it? A swamp buggy can be pieces of all these things scrambled together in a bizarro monster machine that can slog through swamps and boonies. When they race around the Mile O' Mud at Florida Sports Park, some sink so low that all you can see is the driver's helmet.

NOISE ALERT! Swamp buggy races are LOUD! The winner jumps into the mucky, muddy Sippy Hole—and takes the Swamp Buggy Queen along, gown and all!

Get in the Bowl! (or just watch)

Get it? The Edge!

Not a cereal bowl, silly! It's skateboard talk for a giant empty shallow swimming pool. The Edge Skatepark is on the edge of Fleischmann Park between the mall and the zoo. There are special times for bikes, too, and separate times for beginners.

Good for walking, too!

Hop on Your Bike!

We think Gordon River Greenway is Naples' best family bike path ever! As you pedal along, watch for a great horned owl, a raccoon or even a fox! Rent a bike at one of Naples' bike shops or bring your own. If you join a group with **Naples Bicycle Tours**, they provide the bikes, helmets, water and snacks. There are shady rest stops along the Greenway, which goes all the way from the Zoo and the Conservancy to Old Naples.

Bounce!

When you're so full of energy you want to jump right out of your skin, head straight to Bounce! Trampoline Sports. There are laser light shows, separate trampoline sections and foam pits for all ages, and—for the big kids—glow-in-the-dark slam dunk basketball and dodgeball.

 Party alert!

Caronchi Photography

Squish-alicious foam pit in the padded Bounce! Jr. Zone

Go Glow Bowling!

Headpinz Entertainment Center glows, sizzles and vibrates like an electrified crayon box. There's laser tag, aerial ropes, a mega game zone, and our favorite, glow bowl. Younger kids might like the 8-lane boutique bowl at their other location, Bowland Beacon.

Saddle Up!

Even first-time riders as young as six love the gentle horseback tour with **M&H Stables.** It's next to the Picayune Strand State Forest, so you may spot a shy deer, or a gator in the lake. After your tour, you can paint the horse and give it a treat. (Horse gets a carrot. Human gets a popsicle!)

Awww! A tiny Shetland pony for the littlest rider!

The Revs Institute

Rev it Up!

1966 Porsche 906 Carrera. 1974 Jorgensen Eagle. 1966 Ford GT40. 1995 McLaren F1. If these cars get your heart racing, head straight to The Revs Institute! See more than 100 famous race cars, like the **first Ferrari to race in the United States.** The race cars are right out in the open so you can **see every amazifying detail. Best for older kids.**

QUIZ
What is racecar spelled backwards?
a. school bus
b. airplane
c. racecar

answer: c

you need reservations!

Get a Hole in One!

At Coral Cay Adventure Golf, you'll **putt through a cave,** a coral reef and **waterfalls** on two 18-hole mini-golf courses.
Hey Birthday Kid: If you have your party here, you get a whole year of free mini golf!

5th Avenue South

When archaeologists started digging around **5th Avenue South, Naples' most famous shopping street,** guess what they found? A two thousand year-old Calusa Indian canoe trail! It was a shortcut from Naples Bay to the Gulf of Mexico, and it still is. You won't see **fierce warriors** anymore (unless maybe if you come to Spooktacular for Halloween) but there are so many **cool shops** for kids and grownups, **funky street sculptures** to discover, and yummylicious food places to try. Things get outrageously fun when they close off the whole Avenue for a **parade** or **free festival.** And wait till you see what happens at Christmas!

5th Ave. S. Business Development District

On the Stage and in The Street

Do you love to dance, act, or play music? Kids like you perform around Naples all year! Catch **KidzAct Youth Theatre** shows at Sugden Community Theatre and the **Naples Youth Orchestra** at **Artis—Naples.** Laugh your head off at the **Naples Players'** family Comedy Night. Go to a weekend matinee at TheatreZone, check out the family-friendly shows at **Gulfshore Playhouse,** or maybe even see a comedic (funny) opera at Opera Naples.

↗ has sensory friendly shows!

"Whar be the sails on that ship?"

Patrice Shields/Naples Players

Seg-WHAT?

A Segway is a two-wheeled motorized thingy that's smaller than a bicycle and easier than a skateboard. You ride standing up, balancing like a gyroscope. (Puh-leez don't ask how a gyroscope works). Big kids over 12 can try it at **Segway of Naples Tours** or **Extreme Family Fun Spot.**

Cambier Park
At the Corner of Huuuuge and Awesome

Great selfie spot with
King Triton and the mermaid!

Where is it? Smack in the middle of downtown beside 5th Avenue South.

What's there? Slides, swings and climbing structures, even a rope bridge and a dragon to climb on!

There's a fun water spray pole to cool off, and plenty of shade under the giant trees. From October to May there's music in the band shell. There are art shows and festivals and free holiday performances, too!

At one end of the park is the Norris Center, where you can see a play or hear a concert, or play ping pong in the game room. At the other end is the big Arthur L. Allen Tennis Center with lots of shady courts, and even kid-friendly Red Ball courts and equipment.

Ever been Geocaching? It's the world's largest treasure hunt! There are hundreds of geocaches around Naples, Marco & The Everglades, including 5th Avenue South and Cambier Park. Get the free app at geocaching.com.

The Florida State Parks Kids GeoTour is way cool. Inside each cache is a nature card. Find them all and win a Geocoin. Check it out at Wiggins Pass State Park, Collier-Seminole State Park, or Fakahatchee Strand State Preserve. We've heard that one of them contains dinosaur poop!

We're pretty sure it's "pretend poop!"

Central Bark

Cambier Park has all kinds of of interesting stuff for your furry buddies to sniff, and plenty of fun for your pooch **on a leash.** But dogs can **romp around off-leash** at nearby **Central Bark,** the City of Naples Dog Park. A tag is required, but it's free.

3rd Street South

"Is that a hot dog over there? Arrrg"

It's the pet-friendliest street in town! They say any pet is welcome—even your pet llama! Dogs love making friends and getting doggie treats at the Saturday farmer's market. They even have their own costume parade in January.

Snow in Florida? Yes!

But only during the winter holidays! For more than a month, 3rd Street South is a magical wonderland. At the lighting of the great tree, snow falls in your hair and on your nose. The Fairy Snowmother, the Snow King and Santa Claus arrive on a fire truck—and they love to be in your pictures.

Sail Like a bazillionaire! aboard the Naples Princess

How cool to sail on the 105-foot fancy motor yacht **Naples Princess!** You'll pass by the Port Royal mansions as you sail around the very tip of Naples and into the Gulf of Mexico. Of course, you *could* watch for **dolphins** and **sea birds** through the big windows inside on the main deck, but it's way more fun to go to the **top deck.** Maybe you can help the captain steer the boat! Pick a daytime cruise or a sunset cruise. You can even have lunch or dinner on board. The Princess sails from **Port O Call Marina.**

Cool Idea!

Invite all the aunts, uncles, cousins and grandparents for a family reunion or an **extra-special birthday party!**

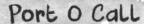

Port O Call

is also a great place to rent a **family-size sightseeing boat.** Or go on a **private fishing trip** or **eco-charter** aboard the **Ms. B. Haven** with that salty ol' fishing guide, **Capt. Mike Bailey.**

Courtesy photo

A Tin City?

Once upon a time, oyster and clam boats chugged up to the docks to unload their catch. Their **oyster-shucking shacks** smelled **pretty stinky**. When the factories closed, someone had the idea to paint the **tin shacks** bright colors, name it **Tin City** and make it a **bizarro place to shop** and eat. Luckily, the shacks **smell like lunch** and cookies instead of stinky oyster shells.

Shop for **outrageous souvenirs** like magic tricks, chocolate alligators, and who knows what else. Walk along the docks and **watch the boats** come in.

On Saturday mornings, **kids sail free** on the **Double Sunshine's** super-fun dolphin sightseeing cruise. There's a **scavenger hunt** and prizes, too.

Sea creature selfie!

City Dock

Wow! Check out the awesome sailboats and motor yachts at the City Dock on **Crayton Cove!** You can sign up for a **fishing trip**, or watch the fishermen bringing in their catch. Then shop for souvenirs or have lunch (or both!)

What a Catamaran!

Oooh! Aaah! That's what people say when the big **catamaran Sweet Liberty** sails by on its sightseeing, dolphin watching and **shelling cruises**. Sit way up on the bow to watch for dolphins, raptors and **desert islands**. The covered deck has a snack bar and tables to eat lunch or **sort your shells**. If you don't see a dolphin the whole trip, you get to **go again for free!**

Shy Wolves & Screaming Cats!
Two Exotic Animal Sanctuaries

Forget about the Big Bad Wolf!

The rescued wolves and wolf dogs come to the **Shy Wolf Sanctuary** sad and hurt. Here, they get **lots of love** and care, and they **give love right back**. The sanctuary also rescues **prairie dogs**, **coyotes**, **foxes** and other way-cool creatures.

> **Q.** How can you tell a wolf's howl from a coyote's?
>
> **A.** A wolf's howl is longer and deeper!

Why are these places called sanctuaries?

Well, some people try to raise a cute little baby wolf, or a fox, or even a python at home, but then it grows up and isn't so cuddly anymore. Sometimes they abandon these **exotic pets** or keep them in tiny cages and stop loving them. **A sanctuary is a safe place** where they can **live happy lives**. You can **visit these** sanctuaries for **free if you call ahead**.

Native American word means "big screaming cat."

Kowia-WHAT?

Want to hug a **skunk?** Pet an **iguana?** Cuddle with a **python** as tall as you are? You can, at **Kowiachobee Animal Preserve!**

Pot-bellied pigs, tigers, leopards and other **big cats** live here, too, but there's not much screaming going on, except maybe by the **parrots**.

Damaris Gonzalez

Don't worry; **their skunk isn't stinky!**

IMMOKALEE

Rhymes with Broccoli

In the Seminole Indian language, Immokalee means "my home." They once called it Gopher Ridge because there were soooo many gopher tortoises. But with all the other creatures that live in these **swamps, forests, lakes** and **prairielands**, it could have been called Deer Ridge or Gator Ridge …even Bear Ridge!

First, it was the hunting ground of the Calusa Indians, and then the Seminoles, white hunters, pioneers, and ranchers called "**cowmen**". Nobody dared to call them cowBOYS because they're REAL MEN. ← — REAL WOMEN, too!

Now, Immokalee is still mostly **farms, ranches** and awesome **wildlife preserves**.

Wilderness Secret!

Every October, the **Pepper Ranch Preserve** is covered in **sunflowers!** On weekends in the dry season you can camp, go hiking, mountain biking or horseback riding. Bring your own tent, bike or horse, of course!

Old Pioneer Ranch

At the **Pioneer Museum at Roberts Ranch,** check out the cowmen's bunkhouse, sugar cane mill, hide curing house and other ranch buildings, just as they were in pioneer days. Each spring, there's a real cowboy cattle drive from Main Street to Roberts Ranch. There's roping and whip-cracking, alligator wrestling, storytelling, crafts, lots of food and music, and even a petting zoo.

QUIZ

Why are the Cowmen and Pioneers called Crackers?

a. They love Ritz Crackers
b. They love Saltine Crackers
c. Their whips make cracking sounds when they're rounding up cattle

Answer: c

Deep, Dark Forests & Spooky Swamps

A Long, Long boardwalk makes it easy to explore Corkscrew Swamp Sanctuary, the largest strand of old-growth bald cypress on the continent! You'll go through deep, dark forests, over spooky swamps and across wide-open prairies. World Wetlands Day is super-fun with music, crafts, a scavenger hunt, and dip netting for all kinds of squiggly things. Will you spot the alligators hiding in the Lettuce Lake?

Old-growth means hundreds of years old!

"Hey kids! You can't eat THAT lettuce!"

lettuce lake

bald crypress

RJ Wiley

What to watch for: alligators, turtles, snakes, deer, wood storks, raccoons, hawks, ospreys and bald eagles. Maybe even a black bear!

wood stork!

Do you like hiking? CREW Bird Rookery Swamp is a huge wilderness. **Lots of wildlife** live there, so it's definitely NOT a good walk for pets! Be sure to start really early in the morning. At Gate 1, look for wildflowers and butterflies. At Gate 5, you can hike into a cypress dome. What's the admission? Zero!

Eco-Safari!

Ecosafari.com

By Airboat

Go for a thrilling **Airboats & Alligators** ride on **Lake Trafford** through **swampy grasslands**, where tons of gators, **great egrets**, raptors and other creatures **lurk about.**

By Jeep

Take an **Orange Jeep Tour** through the private swamps and prairies still owned by our region's founding family.

or pony-back

On Horseback

Take a guided **trail ride** deep in cowboy country. Imagine sitting around a **bonfire** eating **s'mores** and singing cowboy songs! At **The Stable Life**, you also can **take riding lessons.**

Collier Adventures

Who knew?

Almost all the winter tomatoes grown in America come from Florida farms—especially **Immokalee!** Juicy watermelons, oranges, and other fruits and veggies, too! Families from a **diversity of world cultures** plant and harvest them, and we get to buy them **fresh at farm markets** all around Naples and Marco Island.

Collier-Seminole State Park

Who'd believe such an **awesome wilderness** could be just 17 miles from a modern city? There's a **shady campground** (pets allowed!), biking and **walking trails**, and **bikes**, **kayaks**, **canoes** & **paddleboards** to rent.

You can go to a free *Junior Ranger program*, take a guided tour on the **Blackwater River**, and even go **stargazing** with **astronomers**!

Check out this *Calusa dugout canoe*, and the **weird walking dredge** that chomped up **rocks and mud** in the Everglades to build the Tamiami Trail.

COLLIER-SEMINOLE
FLORIDA PARK SERVICE
STATE PARK
20200

mud and rock chomper!

Polka-dot Batfish?

Kevin Bryant

Imagine a triangle-shaped, polka-dotted fish with legs that looks like a **bat with warts**, with lipstick-colored lips, and a fishing lure growing out of her head. There she is, walking along the sandy seagrass bed with that lure wiggling away. All of a sudden, a delicious-looking shrimp swims by. She puckers up those red lips and **whoosh**... lunch! **True or false?**

If you said "true," you're right! And that's not the only outrageous creature living in the **Rookery Bay National Estuarine Research Reserve**. The humongous **mangrove estuary** is home to gazillions of birds and animals. At the **Environmental Learning Center**, you can see the **skulls** and **bones** of all kinds of wildlife, and touch **live horseshoe crabs** and other sea creatures in the big interactive aquarium. Outside, look for manatees from the **observation bridge**, or walk the Snail Trail.

Q. What tiny sea creature that lives in Rookery Bay has a head like a **donkey**, a curly tail like a **monkey**, and a pouch like a **kangaroo**?

A. find it on this page!

Rising Tide Explorers

Want to go paddling in the Reserve with real marine biologists? **Rising Tide Explorers** will take you to **secret spots** in the back bay to see what hides in the **mangroves** and under the water. Who might you meet? A **giant snail**? Sea star? Huge conch? Tiny shrimp? **Sea urchin**? Lizardfish? You may even get **eyeball to eyeball** with a **polka-dot batfish**!

conch rhymes with bonk!

Bring the grownups for a whole day of super family fun on Science Saturday, the last Saturday of each month all year. And in summer, **kids** get in **Free** on **Fridays**!

MARCO ISLAND
One Ginormous Pile of Shells

Pete Sottong

Were the **Calusa** Indians really **cannibals?** Nobody knows for sure, but we do know one thing: they ate a *lot* of seafood. How do we know? Because **Marco Island started as a giant pile of clam, oyster and whelk shells!** After a delicious seafood dinner, the Calusas dumped the empty shells into the muddy mangrove roots. A bazillion seafood dinners later, those huge mounds of shells became whole islands. Marco is the largest Calusa Indian **garbage dump** (though it's nicer to say shell mound) in the Ten Thousand Islands. **Best recycling ever!**

What's fun to do on Marco Island? Turn the page and find out!

newborn mangrove island

Bruce Hitchcock

41

Wait! A 1,000-Year-Old Cat?

Well, sort of! The Calusa were fierce, but guess what! They also were very **artistic!** They carved beautiful **masks**, and **sculptures** like this tiny **half-panther, half-human** statue. It was buried in a **mucky bog** on Marco Island for more than a thousand years! The archaeologists who found it called it the Key Marco Cat.

Replicas by Peter Sottong

They took it to the **Smithsonian Institution** in Washington, DC. But the people of Marco wanted to borrow it back for a while, so they built the **Marco Island Historical Museum** to give it a safe home. It's worth about **98 zillion dollars** (or something like that) and has its own security guard!

But that's not all! There are more ancient Calusa carvings, a life-size Calusa village, Calusa tools and weapons made from sharks teeth, deer bones, and sharp shells, a pioneer exhibit, and lots of cool happenings, like Pineapple Day each February!

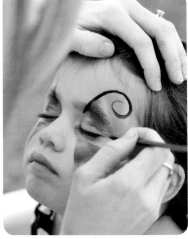

face painting!

10,000 Islands? Who's Counting?

It's impossible! Storms wash some islands away. New mangroves pop up like magic, making new islands. There may be 10,002, or 979, or ten bazillion. Nobody's actually counting. Of course, you're welcome to try. Marco is the biggest of the 10,000 Islands!

#2,968?

sharp shell = Calusa weapon

Abshellutely Fabulous Fun!

Oh, the seashells and **fossils** you can find **mucking around** the secret coves and **mud flats** of the 10,000 Islands! Meet your **Treasure Seekers Shell Tour** guide at the Goodland Boating Park. Bring a snack and extra **dry clothes**!

baby horse conch

whelk

barnacles

seahorse

shark's tooth

worm shell

What's Your Superpower?

If you were a barnacle, you'd crawl around till you find a spot you like, **ooze cement** out of your antennae, and then flip **upside down** and **glue your head** to a shell—and then **stand on your head the rest of your life!** Since you're upside down, you'll be grabbing your food with your feet.

Rob Modys

Go Fish!

Imagine catching a fish as tall as you. Lots of kids do! You can fish all around the 10,000 Islands or go way out in the Gulf of Mexico to look for really huge ones. Marco Island has soooo many great **fishing guides**. Some, like **Old Marco Charter Fishing** and **Native Guided Fishing Charters**, specialize in families.

"A shark's skin is rough like sandpaper—not smooth like mine!"

Get it? Fishing r-e-e-l!

Charter Fishing Information

Q. Who loses more teeth, you or a shark?

A. If you lose more than 30,000 teeth in your life, you win! It's a good thing sharks don't know about the tooth fairy!

Want a Reel Shark Experience?

Try shark fishing with Captain Dakotah of **Dreamlander Tours!** Maybe you'll catch a nurse shark, a blacktip shark, a lemon shark or a bonnethead shark. Okay, **they're not cuddly like puppies**, but once you get to know them you may like them!

Hop on Board at Rose Marina

There are a zillion ways to get on the water: by **yacht** or **catamaran** or **fishing boat**, or even a **pirate ship**. Or, maybe even rent your own **family-size pontoon boat**.

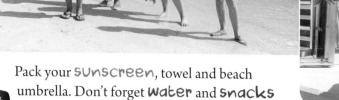

Hemingway Water Shuttle

Pretend you're headed for a desert island, with **clear, shallow water** for swimming and a **soft, white sand** beach where new shells wash up every day. No cars, hotels, restaurants or shops. That's what **Keewaydin Island** is like! Captains Steve and Matt will take you there and pick you up again. Furry First Mate **Riley** helps watch for **jumping dolphins**.

Pack your **sunscreen**, towel and beach umbrella. Don't forget **water** and **snacks** for you and your **doggie**.

*"Thar be **no pirate sailings in summer**, arrrg! Them scallywags be marauding and pillaging on the high seas."*

*"Did somebody say **PIE**?"*

The Black Pearl

Want to join the **scurvy crew** of the Black Pearl? Get your pirate **tattoo** and pirate bandana, and learn how to talk and **dance like a pirate**. Be ready for a **cannon battle** with that scoundrel, **Pirate Pete**. There's grog and **treasure** for all!

Key West Express

Imagine! You can sail from Marco to crazy Key West in three hours on the **triple decker** Key West Express ferry. Have fun all day and come back in the afternoon or stay overnight. Climb to the top of the **lighthouse**. Check out the **roosters strutting** around town. Ride the **Conch Train**, and watch for the **Key Lime Pie Man**, waving as you chug past his shop.

What's on Keewaydin?

Horeshoe crabs!

Not a weapon!

The horseshoe crab uses its tail to **flip itself over** when the waves toss it upside down in the sand.

QUIZ
Horseshoe crabs aren't crabs! They're related to

a) horses

b) spiders

c) stingrays

answer: b

Horseshoe crabs lay **thousands of eggs** that look like **squishy green grapes.** Kind of **like spider eggs!**

Dunes!

Railroad vine! It **grows so fast** you can almost (but not quite) watch it happen!

Seashells! Remember: take only empty ones and don't forget a **bucket** for your **treasures!**

Awww, a baby horseshoe crab!

Snack Boats!

Pink Ice Cream Boat

Marco Beach

Sorry, No Tigers Here!

Tigertail Beach Park is a fantastical, sun-tacular place to spend a day. There are **paddleboards, kayaks** and super-fun **water trikes** to rent, a **playground**, picnic tables and **grills**, beach cabanas, a **snack bar** and showers. There's even a **butterfly garden**! But what's with the crazy name? Well, Tigertail is an **important Native American name**, including **Chief Tigertail** of the **Seminole** tribe, and **Buffalo Tiger**, a founder of the **Miccosukee** tribe.

Tony Smith

Shutterstock

When you take a boardwalk over the dunes, you might spot a **gopher tortoise** or maybe even an **amazifying spiny-tailed iguana**. Don't worry, iguanas are **vegetarians** and wouldn't find you at all tasty!

Tony Smith

Scooping up lunch with their "spoon" bills!

Beautiful Spit

Not that kind of spit! "Spit" also means **a piece of land** sticking out from the mainland, like **Sand Dollar Spit** at Tigertail Beach. You can **wade or kayak across** a shallow lagoon to **go shelling** on the beautiful white sand beach. Maybe you'll find a **sand dollar!**

Fun!

What Does the Sea Bird See?

Wouldn't you just love to **sprout some wings and fly** over the Gulf of Mexico?

We would, too! Do the next best thing and go parasailing! You drift oh–so–gently above the water. You might see manatees or dolphins playing, or a pelican diving for its lunch. Try it **with your grownups, your BFF** or even all by yourself!

Sign up for your parasailing, a **sighteeing cruise** or **waverunner tour** at **Marco Island Watersports.**

Shady Secret: Polarized sunglasses help you see fish, manatees and dolphins under the water better than regular ones!

Beachiest 4th of July Festival Ever!

The **free all-day Marco beach party** has sack races, three-legged races, patriotic swimsuit contests, hula hooping, limbo, and sandcastle-building contests. And, of course, **fireworks!**

KEEP OUT
BIRD NESTING AREA
Bird Nesting Areas Are Protected By State and Federal Law. Do Not Enter This Area.

Please tiptoe around (not in!) the **protected bird nesting areas.**

Eco-Tours and Wacky Human Buzzards

Ron Hagerman

Sociable Show-offs

Humans love dolphins, and when we treat them respectfully, they certainly seem to love us back. **Capt. Ron's Awesome Everglades Adventures** or **Avi's Watersports** can take you to spots where these friendly show-offs love to jump and play. Maybe a sweet, curious manatee will swim up to say "hi."

Would you rather make creature friends by **private boat tour**? Check out the super family-friendly **Marco Island Boat Tours** or **Florida Saltwater Adventures**. Or take a catamaran ride with **Off the Hook Adventures** or **Cool Beans Cruises**.

Ted E. Johnson Jr.

Yak Yak Yak

Kayak, that is. Or **canoe**, or **paddleboard**. But **positively no motors** are allowed at Capri Paddlecraft Park! Meet your Paddle Marco tour guide here to explore the **oh-so quiet** places where birds, **raccoons** and other creatures live. First time paddling? No worries—it's easy!

Buzzard Lope Princess

Wacky Human Buzzards

The tiny fishing village of Goodland is **a little odd.** Actually, a lot odd. Where else do ordinary people jump onto a stage and dance like buzzards? At the **Mullet Festival** each January, women and girls dress in outrageous feather costumes at Stan's Idle Hour Restaurant and do the **Buzzard Lope**, hoping to be crowned Buzzard Lope Queen and Princess.

Mostly, Goodland is an excellent place for eco-tours, fishing charters and un-fancy seafood restaurants.

Be A Dolphin Researcher

*"We dolphins have such **strong tail fins** that we can actually **stand up on the water!**"*

It's true! You can be part of the important 10,000 Islands Dolphin Research Project. The research crew aboard Dolphin Explorer studies about 200 dolphins in the estuaries around Marco Island. Can you guess how you'll recognize them? By the shape and marks on their dorsal fins, and sometimes by scrapes and scars. You might see some of the new baby dolphins with their moms. If you discover a new member of the pod, you get to name it!

The three-hour expedition stops at the beach for shelling and swimming, and you get an official Dolphin Researcher patch.

Captain Kent & his researchers

torn dorsal fin

Kent Morse

True or false? A dolphin is always smiling.

If you said false, you're right! That "smile" is just how its jaw is designed.

Freaky Factoid #1
If a shark bites a dolphin, too bad for the shark. All it gets is a big mouthful of blubber! Also, dolphins can regrow their skin 300 times faster than humans!

Freaky Factoid #2
A dolphin is not a fish. It's a toothed whale, and it breathes air just like us!

Strange Case of the Disappearing Domes

Alien spacecraft? Giant concrete mushrooms?

1989

What are those bizarre white igloo-things poking out of the water at Cape Romano? Surprise! There used to be more of them, all connected, making one big, wonderful house on a wide sandy beach.

What happened? Hurricanes and erosion! Go see them before they disappear into the sea forever!

2015

2018

Bald Eagles?

Look way UP!

There's a bald **eagle nest** in the **Marco Island Nature Preserve** and **Eagle Sanctuary!** We keep our talons crossed that new baby **eaglets** will be born in the nest each winter. A **hidden camera** up there from September to May lets us watch the eggs **hatch** and see the new babies grow.

Kathy Kochanowski

Burrowing Owls?

Look way DOWN!

The **cutest little owls** we ever saw live in sandy **burrows** (kind of **like rabbit holes!**) all over Marco Island. You can see them on the ground or **staring at you** from little **wood perches**. Go ahead and stare right back, but please stay on the edge of the property **so they don't get scared.**

Karen DiNoto

Camp Like a Pirate!

What's it like to camp out like the Calusas, pirates and hermits? Why not try it? **Tent camping is free** on **several islands** in the Rookery Bay Reserve and in the 10,000 Islands. Will you find a **Calusa weapon** or a **Spanish doubloon?**

*"Heard tell that the **fancy-pants French pirate** Jean Laffite buried **plenty of treasure** in these parts."*

QUIZ
What's a pirate's favorite letter?

1) rrrr
2) X
3) The C (get it?)

Answer: 2 because X marks the spot!

See Manatees!

Take a slow, easy boat ride through manatee habitats with **Double R's Fishing and Tours** or **Manatee Sightseeing Eco Adventures** at Port of the Islands Marina. Their nature-friendly deck boats are just right for families.

Manatee nose!

Shoot Hoops! Get Sprayed! Play Frisbee with the Dog!

There's lots for kids to do at Mackle Community Park.

Big kids: hit the game room, basketball court, or sand volleyball court.

Little kids: head for the Kids' Cove playground and water spray park.

ALL kids (and grownups too): ride your bike! See a free outdoor movie! Unleash your fur buddy in the Canine Cove Dog Park.

Go for a Movie and a Taco

You can watch the movie while eating your spaghetti... or pizza, or broccoli, or whatever you like... at Marco Movies.

Play Mini Golf

Putt through the pretty gardens and waterfalls at Marco Golf & Garden.

Hear Spooky Stories

Is it true about pirate curses and ghosts on Marco Island? Maybe so; maybe not. Decide for yourself on the **Marco Mystery & History Tour.** Best for age 13 and up.

Go WILD on the Water!

Zoom around like a motorcycle on water in a personal watercraft. Only grownups can drive at FULL Throttle Waverunners, but even really little kids love to ride.

THE EVERGLADES

Alligators & Panthers & Bears, Oh My!

They call it **The Last Frontier**, and wait until you find out why! This **enchanted wilderness** has many secrets, like a beautiful **white ghost** that's not the least bit spooky and raptors descended from dinosaurs. It's a wild place where alligators, panthers and bears live free, and that **brown water** in the **cypress swamp** tastes dee-licious – honest!

You can **paddle through mysterious mangrove tunnels,** rumble through the outback on a swamp buggy, or fly like the wind across the water in a wild airboat ride. Is that all? No way! Put on your adventure hat and **follow these panther tracks to the next page and find out!**

Dennis Axer

53

A River of Grass

Shutterstock

So here you are in the Everglades!

There's no place else like it on the planet. **Who lives here?** About **57 trazillion** creatures! Also, the **Seminole Indians**, the only **Native American tribe** that was never defeated by the U.S. government! That's why they're called the **Unconquered People!**

Cabbage palm hammock

more hammocks

Dry season is gold

Wet season is green

Don't sleep in this hammock! (unless you're a **panther** or something)

In scientist-talk, a hammock is higher land in the middle of **wet marsh.**

A newspaper reporter named **Marjory Stoneman Douglas** came up with the perfect name for the Everglades: **River of Grass.** You can see why! She did more than anyone in history to **save the Everglades** from being destroyed.

Q. Does the Everglades have seasons?

A. **Absotively, Posilutely, yes!**
Summer rains keep the prairies as green as **Kermit the Frog.** In dry winter months, it turns golden! Which color is more **splendiferous? Whoa, tough question!**

Indian fry bread!

Seminoles!

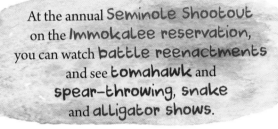

How would you like to **meet descendants** of **brave Seminole warriors**, see their ceremonies and hear their stories? At **Ah-Tah-Thi-ki Museum**, take the interpretive **boardwalk** into a **shady cypress dome** to the **ceremonial grounds** and **living village**. Inside the museum are awesome artifacts and life-size models of **Seminole ancestors**. In November, you can watch **dances**, taste yummy **Indian tacos** and **fry bread** and more at the **American Indian Arts Celebration**.

At the annual **Seminole Shootout** on the **Immokalee reservation**, you can watch **battle reenactments** and see **tomahawk** and **spear-throwing, snake** and **alligator shows**.

Spoiler alert! The Indians win.

How many Alligators?

Counting alligators in the Everglades is about 100 times harder than counting the 10,000 Islands. And guess what! It's the only place on earth where **alligators** and **crocodiles** share the **same habitat.**

"But we're not exactly BFFs!"

I bazillion and one

I bazillion and two

I bazillion and three

Dan Laursen/Wooten's

Q. What's the difference between an alligator and a crocodile?

A. An alligator will **see you later.** A crocodile will see you **after a while.**

Just kidding.

Wish you could rumble and roll through the forest in a swamp buggy, meet a family of deer and see an **old pioneer swamp camp,** and then **hug a baby alligator?** At **Wooten's Everglades Airboat Tours,** you can do ALL those things, plus you can watch a fearless **alligator wrestler** put his face inside the **creatures' jaws,** and even get practically **face to face** with **slithering alligators** yourself!

Why did the gator cross the road?

To get to the gator on the other side!

Airboats and Swamp Buggies!

If a swamp buggy is a **hi-larious mishmash** of **engines** and **truck parts** sitting way up on **monster truck tires**, then what's an airboat made of? Some of the same kinds of parts, but it sits on a **flat boat** instead of wheels. You'll recognize an airboat by its **giant propeller** inside a **metal cage!**

Corey Billie's is the airboat attraction **closest to Naples** and **Marco Island**. The Billie family are descendants of a Seminole chief. There are **lots more airboat rides** along U.S. 41 through the Everglades. And especially **Everglades City**, which is **airboat heaven!** Look for the signs: **Speedy's, Captain Jack's, Jungle Erv's, Captain Mitch's,** and more!

FAST & NOISY Alert!

Meet the Gladesmen of Florida's Last Frontier

The first **pioneers** in the Everglades called themselves **Gladesmen**. They **hunted alligators** and fished (and made **moonshine**, too!). They lived in camps deep in alligator-infested **swamps**, **hammocks** and **prairies**. How did they get around? **Pole boats** and **swamp buggies**! For a real Gladesman tour into the wilderness, check out **Captain Steve's Swamp Buggy Adventures** or **Everglades Adventure Tours**.

really shallow water!

pole boat!

Everglades Adventure Tours

swamp buggy

Fakahatchee
(rhymes with **back-scratchy!**)

You know about the Amazon rainforest, right? It's the largest rainforest on the planet. Well, **Fakahatchee Strand** is called **America's Amazon**. It has **open prairies** and mysterious bald cypress swamps with twisty vines. **Slogging** through the **swamp** is super-fun in summer when the cool, clear water can come **up to your middle!** Even grownups love it! In winter, it's pretty dry.

Another way to stay dry is the **Big Cypress Bend boardwalk**. At the end, you can look down into a **deep, dark alligator hole!** It's on U.S. 41 **next to the Indian Village**, and it's **free!**

A Ghost in the Swamp

People come to Fakahatchee Strand Preserve State Park from all over the world to look for the super-rare ghost orchid. It's called "ghost" because it's white and floaty-looking. It also looks like a tiny ballerina. She usually blooms only once a year, but sometimes she makes an extra appearance! Check out the naturalist-guided swamp walks.

Swamp Angels
(that's a mosquito joke)

If you're exploring some parts of the 'glades in summer without your repellant, you definitely won't be calling these annoying creatures angels. But guess what! Mosquitoes don't hang out in cypress swamps because certain plants, fish and dragonflies like to eat them. Dragonflies are the real angels!

QUIZ

A dragonfly eats

a. dragons, of course!
b. no-see-ums
c. swamp angels

Answer: b and c

Deer Alert!

Janes Scenic Drive is an old dirt logging road in Fakahatchee Strand. Look for alligators, snakes and great blue herons. In the early morning or late afternoon, you may see a raccoon or even a deer out for a stroll.

Big Cypress Swamp

4,500 miles from the North Pole!

Whoever heard of having **waaay too much fun?** Head into the Big Cypress National Preserve and find out! You can **camp**, go **hiking, kayaking** or **canoeing**; be a **Junior Ranger**; look for **deer, panthers**, and even **bears!** Start at the Big Cypress Swamp **Welcome Center. It's free!**

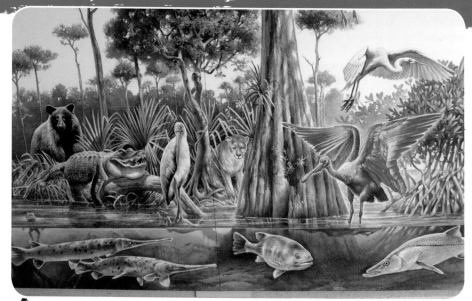

Bears in Florida? Naaaah.

Oh yes! Even with those **fur coats**, black bears **LOVE** the nice, warm Everglades. When you go on a wilderness adventure, be sure to **look up in trees** and watch for **tracks** on the **trail.** What do bears eat? Mostly fruit, berries and bugs. That's good for them. But **people picnics are bad** for them and definitely not safe for people.

So don't leave a **single crumb** behind!

Can smell things seven times better than a bloodhound!

mm mm, tasty!

Stargazing

Attention future **astronauts** and **astronomers!** On super-dark nights, the **Everglades Astronomical Society** sets up **gigantic telescopes** to look at **meteors, planets & nebulas.** They have ladders so even little kids can see!

Get Wet and Wild!

What's the **best excuse** in the **whole world** to get **muddy?** Put on your grungy old sneakers and long pants for a **Wet & Wild Swamp Walk!** Who knows what you'll discover growing and **living in the shadows!** You'll need to bring a change of clothes.

Swamp: Clyde Butcher Gallery   Flower: Susan Rohl

Whoa: What's that Scary Sound?

If you hear **really loud, scary grunts** coming from the swamp, it may not be what you think. It could be a little **pig frog.** For real! The mamas lay **10,000 eggs** at a time, so no wonder there's so much noise!

Best Scenic Roads in Big Cypress

All kinds of **wildlife** hang out on **Loop Road** (27-mile ride) and **Turner River Road** (17-mile ride). The gravel roads sometimes get flooded in summer. Find out the conditions at the Welcome Center.

Bumpy ride alert!

"Don't forget! The best times to see us are early morning and late afternoon."

Meet Some Manatees

no neck!

Frank Brinker

After you check out the **cool exhibits** in the Welcome Center, go outside to the **boardwalk** and look for **manatees** in the canal. They especially like to hang out in the **warm water** here in winter.

A manatee **can't turn its head** sideways, so it must flip its **whole body** around to look at you.

The Tree's Knees

What are those **pointy things** poking out of the water beside the cypress trees? Cypress knees! Some scientists think they shoot up from the tree's roots to **help it breathe,** kind of **like a snorkel!**

Everglades City

Buggy-est job ever!

After Barron Collier built a **hunting** and **fishing lodge** in the **wilderness**, there was one serious problem: **no road!** So he hired **2,000 men** to **dig** through the **swamps.** Then he decided to build a fancy town. It's not fancy anymore, and that's a good thing! Now the **The Rod & Gun Club** is a way-cool restaurant, the **bunkhouse** is a motel (**The Ivey House**), and the **laundry building** is the Museum of The Everglades. You won't believe some of the outrageous pioneer tales and **artifacts** there.

And it's **free!**

One Claw Only!

Everglades City is the **stone crab capital of the world!** But you don't eat the whole crab! The fishermen must take only one claw, and then **release the crab** back into the water to **grow a new one.**

Are you in the mood for **fresh fish,** juicy **oysters,** blue crab, or **Everglades specialties** like **gator nuggets** and fried **frog legs?** You're definitely in the right town!

"Umm, not a fan!"

STEAMED SHRIMP
DINNERS WRAPS
SALADS
CRAB CAKES
STONE CRABS
ICE CREAM

Who's brave enough to taste?

Everglades National Park Starts In Everglades City

Mitchell B. Thompson

Plumes!

A hundred years ago when ladies wore **outrageous bird-feather hats,** hunters killed **five million egrets** and **roseate spoonbills** in the Everglades. Now they're protected. **No shooting**—except with your **camera!**

Supercolonies!

After the **plume-hunting** stopped, birds started coming back. Some flocks, like **white ibis,** are so **plentiful** that they're called **supercolonies.** And wait till you see the **giant white pelicans** with **wingspans** as long as a **car!**

To see the **sandbars** and **rookeries** where the **wading birds** hang out, go on a **naturalist-guided kayak** or **boat tour.** You also can go **hiking, biking, camping,** and of course, **fishing!**

Get maps and information at the **Gulf Coast Visitor Center,** and be sure to check out the **guides, outfitters, restaurants** and places to stay at **florida-everglades.com.**

QUIZ

Roseate spoonbill feathers are pink because they

a. drink pink lemonade
b. eat pink shrimp
c. stay too long in the sun

Answer: b

Hey 4th Graders!

4TH GRADER ACCESS
ALL FEDERAL LANDS AND WATERS

For one whole year, you and your family can get a **FREE PASS** to all **national parks,** lands and waters. Download it at EveryKidinAPark.gov.

4 feet tall

2 feet tall

Cynthia Gilbert kayakSWFL.com

#1 Fishing Spot in the World!

what do you think?

Is a **million acres of water** where the Ten Thousand Islands meets Everglades National Park enough to find the most **amazifying fish** of your life? Some fishermen say this is the **most excellent fishery** on the planet. Why? Because nothing disturbs their habitat! We like **catch, take picture-and-release,** but that's up to you.

Best fishing guides too!

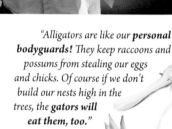

No Free Lunch Charters

Chokoloskee Charters

"Alligators are like our **personal bodyguards!** They keep raccoons and possums from stealing our eggs and chicks. Of course if we don't build our nests high in the trees, the **gators will eat them, too.**"

Walking islands

Be **whisper-quiet** as you kayak with your expert guide into the **hidden tunnels** and lagoons of the 10,000 Islands. Some of the tunnels are so low and narrow that you have to **duck your head** to get through! **Getting sooo close** to **gators, raccoons,** and beautiful **birds** may be the **highlight** of your **whole year!** It's better than storybook land, because it's real! Check out **Everglades Area Tours, Shurr Adventures,** or **Jenny's Eco Everglades Wilderness Tours.**

Don't these red mangrove roots look like **humongous spiders or bird legs walking** through the creek? Ask your guide to explain how they really do walk!

RJ Wiley

Here's the thing: Gators aren't really being nice guys. All that **bird poop** dropping into the water **feeds the fish** they love to eat.

Old Trading Post

100 years ago, Chokoloskee Island was like the **Wild West**. Gladesmen, Indians and hermits came by boat and dugout canoe to **Ted Smallwood's trading post** to trade their animal **furs**, hides and alligator meat for flour, **medicine** and **supplies**. Smallwood Store is a **museum** now, but it feels just like it did then. You'll even see **old Ted, still sitting** in the rocking chair he loved when he was alive.

People say the store is haunted by the ghosts of Ted, pirates and outlaws … maybe even that hermit, Juan Gomez. Movie crews are always coming around, hoping to film a ghost. In the gift shop you can sign up for the **Smallwood Store Boat Tour** to visit the birds' favorite rookeries and **sandbars**.

On a boat-assisted kayak tour, your boat takes you and your kayaks to some outer islands where you'll paddle through **secret passages** and **muck around** in the **mud flats** for tiny snails, giant whelks and other creatures.

"Like hermit crabs!"

Do you see what we see?

Everglades Area Tours

You're headed here

Super fun guide

Fast boat

Everglades Area Tours.com   239-695-3633

Your kayak goes here

You ride here

Clyde Butcher

is the world's most famous **Everglades photographer.** He loves sloshing around taking pictures in the **Big Cypress Swamp.** You can join one of his super-fun naturalist-guided walks that start right behind his **Big Cypress Gallery.** People who really, **really** love the swamp can even rent his **personal swamp cottage for a vacation,** where the backyard critters are alligators.

Clyde Butcher Gallery

Smallest Post Office

This teeny, tiny post office is **smaller than a backyard playhouse!** Only **one person** can fit inside **at a time!** It's on U.S. 41 in Ochopee.

Best Camping Trip Ever!

Your Everglades camping guide will take you by boat or kayak to one of the 10,000 Islands, set up camp, cook, and do all the work. What's your job? To have fun! Check out two of our faves, **Captain Don McCumber** or "**Kayak Cynthia**" **Gilbert** at Kayak SW Florida.

Miccosukee Festival

The Miccosukee Indian Village is closer to Miami than to Naples, but it's fun to visit during their Indian Arts and Crafts Festival each December. Lots of alligator wrestling, native dancing, Indian food, art, crafts and Indian-guided airboat rides.

SWAMP TALK

weird job alert: Head Skunk Ape Researcher!

Skunk Ape? For Real?

Do you **believe in Bigfoot?** Well, this 7-foot-tall, 350-pound ape that **smells like a skunk** could be its Everglades cousin. It **stinks** because it wallows around in alligator holes (which are full of **swamp gas**), **never bathes,** and eats too many Lima beans.

You can go on a swamp expedition or other land or water adventure with **Everglades Adventure Tours. Truth alert:** No skunk ape sightings are likely, but you could get an official skunk ape T-shirt at the **Skunk Ape Headquarters** gift shop.

Uh, Really??

Pythons? Yep! Huge Ones!

Not good. Invasive species.

There are thousands of Burmese pythons in the Everglades, but hardly anybody sees one in the wild because they stay hidden. Goldie, here, is 30 feet long and **weighs 300 pounds**. She lives at the Skunk Ape Headquarters.

Chickee: it's not what you might think

NOT!

Many Seminole and **Miccosukee Indians** still live in traditional open-sided **huts** with **palmetto palm** roofs. Most chickees around Naples, Marco Island and the Everglades, like this one at **Trail Lakes Campground**, were built by tribe members. Or you can have a sleepover in a chickee at **Billie Swamp Safari**.

Who wants to sleep in the loft?

WHAT'S UP THE ROAD?

If you've played yourself silly and done every single thing in this book, take a drive up to Sanibel Island, the world's most famous shelling beach. Or try something else on this page!

"Every single thing? **Impossible!"**

Bonita Springs

Go Bat Crazy!

When the moon is full, go on a Batmoon Paddle with CGT Kayaks. Watch 1,000 Brazilian free-tailed bats whoosh out from under their bridge at sunset for a bug-a-licious feast.

Meet Zeus and Buddha

Everglades Wonder Gardens is one of the wonkiest Old Florida roadside attractions. Zeus, the land tortoise, has a rooster for a roommate and a blue-faced iguana named Buddha for a neighbor. Plus, a whole lot of gators and flamingos, and other weird birds.

Go on a Golf Safari

...in the deepest, darkest jungles of Africa at Congo River Golf or Golf Safari Minigolf.

Estero

Cool off on the Ice

Friday is family skate night at Hertz Arena, home of the minor league ice hockey team, the Florida Everblades.

Camp & Kayak on the Estero River

Sign up at Koreshan State Park. Some very smart but totally wacky pioneers once lived there. They thought that the earth is like a shell and people live inside. There's an interesting museum, some pioneer buildings, and fun ranger events.

Fort Myers

Peek Into Thomas Edison's Laboratory

Yes, his real laboratory, plus his house and about a gazillion of his inventions. You might even see the *pretend* Thomas Edison or his neighbor, Henry Ford, walking around the Edison & Ford Winter Estates.

Meet Baseball Stars

Meet the big stars of the Boston Red Sox and the Minnesota Twins during spring training at Hammond and Jet Blue stadiums. Root for the home team, the Fort Myers Miracle, all summer.

Sway says hi!

FESTIVALS! FAIRS! PARADES!

January

Southwest Florida Nature Festival, Rookery Bay **m**

Martin Luther King Day Parade, 5th Avenue S. **n**

New Year's Art Fair, 5th Avenue S. **n**

Mullet Festival, Goodland **m**

Pets on Third, 3rd Street S. **n**

Chalk Art on Fifth Avenue **n**

February

Pineapple Day, Marco Island Historical Museum

Everglades City Seafood Festival

World Wetlands Day, Corkscrew Swamp Sanctuary **n**

Strawberry Festivals **n,b**

Woofstock **n**

Helen Bryan, Everglades City Seafood Festival

March

Marco Island Seafood & Music Festival

St. Patrick's Day Parade, Old Naples

Kids Fishing Clinic, Naples Pier

Immokalee Cattle Drive & Jamboree **i**

Seminole Shootout Battle Reenactment **i**

Collier County Fair **n**

April

Earth Day Festival, Conservancy of SWFL **n**

Florida Gopher Tortoise Day, Naples Preserve

Taste of Collier, Bayfront **n**

Taste of Marco, Esplanade **m**

Pinwheels at the Pier **n**

Naples = **n**   Marco Island = **m**   Everglades = **e**   Immokalee = **i**   Bonita Springs/Estero = **b**

SUMMERTIME HAPPENINGS!

May

Naples CityFEST, Downtown

Mother's Day! Moms get in free at many attractions!

Free Family Community Day, Artis - Naples ⋒

Special Olympics SUP-Luau Races ⋒

Summertime

Awesome summer discounts and freebies for kids!

Free summer movies, theaters around town

Gone Fishing (SummerFest), Naples Pier ⋒

Hot Summer Nights, Sun-N-Fun Lagoon ⋒

June

Father's Day! Dads get in free at many attractions!

Early 4th of July Fireworks, Everglades City

Naples Pride LGBTQ Festival

July

4th of July Parade, Fifth Avenue S. ⋒

4th of July Fireworks, Naples Pier

Uncle Sam's 4th of July Sand Jam & Fireworks, Marco

Ice Cream Social, ski show & fireworks, Sugden Park ⋒

August

A great month to go ice skating, see free movies and visit your fave museums!

September

Grandparents Day! They get in free at many attractions.

Jennifer Brinkman

HOLIDAYS! LIGHTS! CELEBRATIONS!

October

Family Halloween Festival, Koreshan, Estero
Halloween Spooktacular, 5th Avenue S. **n**
Stone Crab Festival **n**
Clyde Butcher's Fall Festival & Swamp Tours **e**
Free Family Community Day, Artis-Naples
Nature Fest, Wiggins Pass State Park **n**
Swamp Buggy Parade and Races **n**

November

Pro Watercross World Championships **n**
American Indian Arts Celebration,
Ah-Tah-Thi-Ki Seminole Museum **e**
Turkey Trot 5K for Kids, Cambier Park **n**
Stories of the Paradise Coast **n**
Grand Illuminations, Santa & snow, Village on Venetian Bay **n**
Florida Panther Festival, Naples Zoo
Christmas Tree Lighting, Veterans' Park **m**
Celebration of Lights and Christmas on 3rd Street S. **n**

December

Community Chanukah Celebration **n**
Tuba Christmas, 5th Avenue S. **n**
Christmas Parade, 5th Avenue S. **n**
Canine Christmas Parade, Esplanade **m**
Marco Island Boat Parade and Street Parade
Naples Boat Parades: Naples Bay and Venetian Bay
New Year's Eve Fireworks, Naples Pier and Sugden Park **n**
Snow Fest Naples
Christmas Walk, Tree Lighting, Performances & Santa, 5th Avenue S. **n**

TELL THE GROWNUPS! Sometimes an event may be either at the end of one month or the beginning of the next month. Check local listings.

Naples = **n**   Marco Island = **m**   Everglades = **e**   Immokalee = **i**   Bonita Springs/Estero = **b**

A bazillion thanks!
To the Warriors and Honorary Warriors of the Mostly Kids' Tribe

WISE ONES

To Jessica Olson, Jack Wert, JoNell Modys and Susan McManus, who believed in the first edition of this book when it was a blank slate and a vision.

To Ed Caum for sharing the vision and opening new doors, and all the other CVB superheroes (Buzzy Ford, Debi DeBenedetto, Michelle Pirre and the rest) who make sure the whole world knows about this amazing place to visit.

And to kindred spirits Stacy Nicolau and Leigh Ann Newman, publishers of Neapolitain Family Magazine, who prove that it's also an awesome place to live.

ART PEEPS

To Margie Olsen for the creation of our newest spokescreatures, Marrrge the Pie-Rat, Freckles the Hermit Crab, Marigold the Sea Turtle, and Allapattah the Baby Alligator.

To Brad Sanders, who first designed Addy-winning advertising campaigns for me years ago (never mind how many).

And to gifted designers Jayla Buie and Christine Rooney for pages spilling over with super-fun whimsey.

KIDSPEAKER & SIDEKICKS

To Sarah Rose Bartlett, whose uncanny ability to see through the eyes of children, advice about delicious healthy food, diversity, inclusion, and up-to-the-minute kidspeak made this book so much better.

To Christopher Bartlett, the most fearless adventurer in my personal tribe, whose positive view and clever ideas inspire me to think bigger, take the risk, and live in the moment.

And to Randy Simmons, my partner in life and mischief-making, for putting another gazillion miles on your odometer and gracefully missing grownup activities to come out and play with the Mostly Kids' Tribe.

Grandmothers & Other Super-Beings

To all the grandparents, parents, aunts, uncles, teachers, home-schoolers, youth leaders, and other grownups who have been asking for this book for so long. Thanks for the inspiration and insights into the hearts and minds of your amazing kids.

And Most Especially

To the many fabulous bookstores, gift shops, childrens' stores and galleries that display and sell the Mostly Kids' Guides.

⭐ STAR ATTRACTIONS

With special thanks to the Leaders of these outstanding family attractions:
Kara Laufer, Amanda Townsend, Karysia Demarest, Jenny Foegen and Charles Wright. You just keep making the Paradise Coast an even more awesome place for families to live and to visit.

Gardens with Latitide

Everglades Boat Tours
Marco Island Boat Tours

A brain-building powerhouse fueled by STEAM
(Science, Technology, Engineering, Art & Mathematics)

The most elegant luxury yacht
in Southwest Florida

On behalf of all our attractions and adventure-makers:
Deepest appreciation to The Naples, Marco Island, Everglades Convention & Visitor's Bureau under the direction of Executive Director Jack Wert for reinforcing Collier County's commitment to family tourism.

Time's A'wastin' Mateys! GET GOING!

A
A & B Charters aandbcharters.com (239) 263-8833
Ah–Tah–Thi–Ki Seminole Indian Museum ahtahthiki.com (877) 902-1113
Airboats & Alligators airboatsandalligators.com (239) 657-2214. See also ecosafari.com
Arthur L. Allen Tennis Center allentenniscenter.net (239) 213-3060
Artis—Naples artisnaples.org (239) 597-1900
Astronomy! Everglades Astronomical Society naples.net/clubs/eas
Avi's Watersports aviwatersports.com (239) 777-9873
AWE All Water Excursions allwaterexcursions.com (239) 594-0213

B
Big Cypress National Preserve nps.gov/bicy (239) 695-2000
Big Cypress Swamp Welcome Center nps.gov/bicy (239) 695-4758
Billie Swamp Safari billieswamp.com (863) 983-6101
Black Pearl Pirate Ship piratesofmarco.com (239) 404-5422
Boston Red Sox Spring Training mlb.com/redsox/spring-training (239) 334-4700
Bounce! Trampoline Sports bouncenaples.com (239) 302-3848
Bowland Beacon bowlandcenters.com (239) 597-3452

C
CGT Kayaks cgtkayaks.com (239) 221-8218
Cabana Dan's cabanadans.com (239) 777-4040
Calusa Spirit marcoislandwatersports.com (239) 642-2359
Captain Don McCumber (See Everglades Area Tours)
Captain Jack's Airboat Tours captainjacksairboattours.com (239) 695-4400
Captain Mitch's captainmitchs.com (800) 368-0065
Captain Ron's Awesome Everglades Adventures evergladesjetskitours.com (239) 777-9975
Captain Steve's Swamp Buggy captainstevesswampbuggyadventures.com (239) 695-2186
Central Bark (City of Naples Dog Park) naplesgov.com (239) 213-7120
Clyde Butcher's Swamp Walks clydebutcher.com (239) 695-2428
C'mon Golisano Children's Museum cmon.org (239) 514-0084
Collier County Museums (all locations) colliermuseums.com
Congo River Golf congoriver.com (239) 948-9099
Conservancy of Southwest Florida conservancy.org (239) 262-0304
Cool Beans Cruises coolbeanscruises.com (239) 777-0020

Coral Cay Adventure Golf coralcaygolf.com (239) 793-4999
Corey Billie Airboat Rides cbairboatrides.com (239) 389-7433
Corkscrew Swamp Sanctuary corkscrew.audubon.org (239) 348-9151
CREW crewtrust.org (239) 657-2253

D
Devlin, Mike kayaktourswithmikedevlin.com (239) 450-2455
Dolphin Explorer dolphin–study.com (239) 642-6899
Double R's Fishing & Tour Co. doublersfishingandtours.com (239) 642-9779
Double Sunshine purenaples.com (239) 263-4949
Dreamlander Tours dreamlandertours.com (239) 331-3775

E–F
Edison & Ford Winter Estates edisonfordwinterestates.org (239) 334-7419
Everglades Adventure Tours evergladesadventuretours.com (561) 985-8207
Everglades Area Tours evergladesareatours.com (239) 695-3633
Everglades Astronomical Society naples.net/clubs/eas
Everglades National Park Gulf Coast Visitor Center nps.gov/ever
Everglades Wonder Gardens evergladeswondergardens.com (239) 992-2591
Extreme Family Fun Spot extremefamilyfunspot.com (239) 774-0061
Florida Saltwater Adventures floridasaltwateradventures.com (239) 595-7495
Fort Myers Miracle miraclebaseball.com (239) 768-4210
Full Throttle WaveRunners fullthrottlewaverunners.com (239) 728-8919

G–H
Golf Safari golfsafariminigolf.com (239) 947-1377
Gordon River Greenway gordonrivergreenway.org
Gulfshore Playhouse gulfshoreplayhouse.org (239) 261-7529
HeadPinz Entertainment Center headpinz.com (239) 455-3755
Hemingway Water Shuttle hemingwaywatershuttle.com (239) 315-1136
Hertz Arena hertzarena.com (239) 948-7825
Holocaust Museum & Education Center holocaustmuseumswfl.org (239) 263-9200

I
In the Pink Ice Cream Boat (Facebook)
Immokalee Pioneer Museum at Roberts Ranch colliermuseums.com (239) 252-2611
Isles of Capri Paddlecraft Park (see rookerybay.org)
Ivey House & Everglades Adventures iveyhouse.com (239) 695-3299

J Jenny's Eco Everglades Wilderness Tours ecoeverglades.com (239) 719-0565

Jungle Erv's Airboat World jungleervairboatworld.com (877) 695-2820

Junior Ranger Programs nps.gov/bicy or floridastateparks.org

Just Beachy Burgers/Just Beachy Food Boat (Facebook)

K "Kayak Cynthia," Kayak The Everglades kayakswfl.wordpress.com (239) 963-7296

Key West Express keywestexpress.net (239) 463-5733

Kowiachobee Animal Preserve kowiachobee.org (239) 352-5387

L Lake Trafford airboatsandalligators.com; ecosafari.com

M M&H Stables mhstables.com (239) 455-8764

Manatee Sightseeing Eco Adventure see–manatees.com (239) 642-8818

Marco Golf and Garden marcogolfandgarden.com (239) 970-0561

Marco Island Boat Tours marcoisland-boattours.com (239) 695-0000

Marco Island Watersports marcoislandwatersports.com (239) 642-2359

Marco Movies marcomovies.com (239) 642-1111

Marco Mystery & History Tour marcomysteryandhistory.com (239) 537-8353

Miccosukee Tribe of Indians miccosukee.com (305) 480-1924

Minnesota Twins Spring Training mlb.com/twins/spring-training (239) 768-4210

Ms. B. Haven fishinnaples.com (239) 825-4292

N Naples Beach Watersports naplesbeachwatersports.com (239) 642-2359

Naples Bicycle Tours naplesbicycletours.com (239) 825-6344

Naples Botanical Garden naplesgarden.org (239) 643-7275

Naples Kayak napleskayakcompany.com (239) 262-6149

Naples Players naplesplayers.org (239) 263-7990

Naples Princess naplesprincesscruises.com (239) 649-2275

Naples Train Museum naplestrainmuseum.org (239) 262-1776

Naples Trolley Tours naplestrolleytours.com (239) 262-7300

Naples Zoo at Caribbean Gardens napleszoo.org (239) 262-5409

Native Guided Fishing Charters nativeguidedfishing.com (239) 285-9252

O Off the Hook Adventures offthehookadventures.com (239) 571-4665

Old Marco Charter Fishing oldmarcocharterfishing.com (239) 289-7228

Old Naples Surf Shop oldnaplessurfshop.com (239) 262-1877

Opera Naples operanaples.org (239) 963-9050

Orange Jeep Tours orangejeeptours.com (239) 434-5337

Paddle Marco paddlemarco.com (239) 777-5423

P

Palm Cottage napleshistoricalsociety.org (239) 261-8164

Panther Festival floridapantherfestival.com (See Naples Zoo)

Paradise Coast Blueway paradisecoastblueway.com

Port O Call Marina portocallmarina.com (239) 774-0479

Port of the Islands Fishing and Tours doublersfishingandtours.com (239) 642-9779

Port of the Islands Manatee Tour see-manatees.com (239) 642-8818

Q-R

Revs Institute revsinstitute.org (239) 687-7387

Rising Tide Explorers risingtidefl.com (239) 734-3231

Rookery Bay Environmental Learning Center rookerybay.org (239) 530-5940

Rose Marina rosemarina.com (239) 394-2502

S

Scuba Marco scubamarco.com (239) 389-7889

Scuba Outfitters Naples scubaoutfittersnaples.com (239) 280-5500

Segway of Naples Tours segwayofnaples.com (239) 262-7300

Seminole Shootout seminoleshootout.com 800-GO-SAFARI

Shurr Adventures Everglades shurradventures.com (239) 300-3004

Shy Wolf Sanctuary shywolfsanctuary.com (239) 455-1698

Six Chuter Charters sixchutercharters.com (239) 389-1575

Skunk Ape Research Headquarters skunkape.info (239) 695-2275

Smallwood Boat Tours smallwoodstoreboattour.com (239) 695-0016

Smallwood Store smallwoodstore.com (239) 695-2989

Speedy's Airboat Tours speedysairboattours.com (239) 695-4448

Sugden Community Theatre naplesplayers.org (239) 434-7340

Sun-N-Fun Lagoon napleswaterpark.com (239) 252-4021

Swamp Buggy Races swampbuggy.com

Sweet Liberty sweetliberty.com (239) 793-3525

T

TheatreZone theatre.zone (888) 966-3352

The Stable Life thestablelifeatavemaria.com (970) 799-4644

Tin City tin-city.com (239) 262-4200

Trail Lakes Campground evergladescamping.net (800) 504-6554

Treasure Seekers Shell Tours treasureseekersshelltours.com (239) 571-2331

U-Z

Up a Creek Kayak Tours upacreekkayak.com (239) 293-6232

Wooten's Everglades Adventures wootenseverglades.com (239) 695-2781

MAJOR BEACHES AND BEACH PARKS WITH FACILITIES

On-site facility phone numbers are listed when available

Barefoot Beach Preserve County Park, Naples | Access gate: 5901 Bonita Beach Road
Clam Pass Beach Park | 465 Seagate Dr., Naples
Delnor-Wiggins Pass State Park | 11135 Gulfshore Dr., Naples (239) 597-6196
Lowdermilk Beach Park 1301 | Gulf Shore Blvd., Naples
Naples Pier 25 | 12th Ave. S., Naples
Tigertail Beach | 490 Hernando Dr., Marco Island (239) 642-8414
Vanderbilt Beach | 100 Vanderbilt Beach Rd., Naples

STATE AND NATIONAL PARKS

National Park Service nps.gov
Florida State Parks floridastateparks.org

COLLIER COUNTY INFORMATION

Collier County Public Library collierlibrary.org (239) 593-0334
Collier County Parks and Recreation colliercountyfl.gov (239) 252-4000
Collier County Museums (all locations) colliermuseums.com
Naples, Marco Island, Everglades Convention & Visitors Bureau paradisecoast.com (239) 252-2384

NAPLES

City of Naples naplesgov.com (239) 213-1000
Naples Parks & Recreation naplesgov.com (239) 213-1000
Greater Naples Chamber of Commerce Visitor Center napleschamber.org (239) 262-6376
Naples Preserve & Hedges Family Eco-Center naplesgov.com (239) 261-4290
Fifth Avenue South fifthavenuesouth.com (239) 692-8436
Third Street South thirdstreetsouth.com (239) 434-6533

MARCO ISLAND

Marco Island Parks & Recreation cityofmarcoisland.com (239) 642-0575

EVERGLADES CITY INFORMATION

Fishing & Eco Guides, Attractions, Hotels, Restaurants florida-everglades.com

About the Author

Karen T. Bartlett is an award-winning author of 12 destination **travel books** and hundreds of **travel articles** and photos in magazines and newspapers in several countries. She is a regular contributor to Gulfshore Life Magazine and **Travel Editor** of **Neapolitan Family** Magazine. She's a member of SATW, the Society of American Travel Writers.

Before becoming an author, she was **president of an Atlanta, Georgia public relations agency.** When her (now grown up) children were small, the family moved to Naples, Florida, and the adventures began! She writes from the point of view of a **reporter**, a **storyteller**, and especially a **mom**. She loves to **dance**, **go shelling**, try **yummy new foods** and hang out with **furry**, **fishy** and **feathery** creatures.

If you LOVED this book...

...**you can have even more splendiferous adventures** and learn more **outrageous stuff** in *A (mostly) Kids' Guide to Sanibel & Captiva Islands and the Fort Myers Coast.*

Important national book award!

You'll get the inside scoop on the most **famous shelling beaches on the planet,** where **gazillions** of **shells** and other creatures (like **purple blobs, angel wings, kitten's paws** and **sharks eyes**) wash up on the sand. Sail to islands where **pirate ships** once battled. Go **zip-lining,** walk a totally awesome **poop trail,** see faraway **galaxies** at the **planetarium,** take your **fur-buddies** to their own private **dog beach** or even to **dog church,** and a **bazillion other things.**

On sale at great bookstores and gift shops all over Southwest Florida

Favorite Things Page

"Every time you do something awesome that you found in the book, write it here! I got you started with one of my favorites."

Love, Rosie the Roseate Spoonbill and all my friends, **Marrge** the Pie Rat, Freckles the Hermit Crab, Allapattah the Baby Alligator, Marigold the Loggerhead Sea Turtle, and Finn the Bottlenose Dolphin.

Where I went	Page	Best Part	Name
Naples Pier	15	Saw two dolphins!	Rosie